Everlasting Chaos

Everlasting Chaos

By:

Fred Sayin

XULON PRESS

Xulon Press
2301 Lucien Way #415
Maitland, FL 32751
407.339.4217

www.xulonpress.com

Printed in the United States of America

Paperback ISBN-13: 978-1-6628-3904-7
Ebook ISBN-13: 978-1-6628-3905-4

Dedication

This book is dedicated to my second scoutmaster: William G. Stoops and my third Scoutmaster Richard Thek and his son Erick who all helped me learn skills to become an Eagle. I still remember learning debating skills to show the reason I was the best person for a leadership position. This society needs to redevelop the skill of debate and not blame as the disciple Paul said: "When I was a child, I thought like a child, now today I have put childish thoughts behind me" Erick Thek showed me what real courage was: He had the guts to run against me for Senior Patrol Leader and he was new to the troop, his father became the new Scoutmaster, nobody in the Scout troop wanted to run against me for my second term of Senior Patrol Leader, so Erick took the challenge. If it wasn't for Erick's display of courage; I would have never earned the Eagle Rank, highest award in Scouts. Plus being in Boy Scouts as a teen has helped me learn many diverse skills that has helped me throughout my life.

Introduction

This book shows consequences for following poor ideas. For example, "defund the police" is like major league baseball not having umpires or the National Football League, not having any referees. The NFL in 2012 had substitute referees as the main referees were on strike. There was such a controversial call, the second week about San Francisco scoring a last second touchdown of a game when it looked like their opposing team intercepted the ball in the end zone. The regular referees were back on the job, the third week of the season. Aren't police responsible for crowd control at football games (both college and pro) and

parades? Couldn't college and pro teams say: "No police, we are not playing, it's too dangerous" OR "since we need to hire a private security team, our ticket prices have to increase" Maybe a parade today that has free admission may have to start charging for tickets. The author of this book believes, all of society needs to hear the problems of "going with the crowd", as the person leading the crowd could have made the biggest mistake and that is a leader in any group as we are all human.

The famous phrase: "If the blind, lead the blind, will they not both fall into a pit"?

Table of Contents

CHAPTER ONE

Be Careful
What You Wish For

I would say: "Defunding the police" is like saying no more referees at NFL games and no more umpires at MLB games. I remember when substitute referees made an unpopular call in a NFL game, where it looked like a pass was intercepted and then went right into the hands of a 49er in the end zone for a last second touchdown. All the angles shown during that game on replay it looked like an interception. At that time, I would have to agree that the substitute referees blew the call, even though the call stood. The following week, the referee strike ended because of that call, the regular referees were back to work at the NFL games, the following week. If society can't deal with poor officiating, how can it deal with no police? Later that season (2012) reviewing the season; I saw the play that the substitute referees blew earlier in the season at a surprise angle and I saw what happened. The defender in the end zone went for the interception, it went through the defender's hands, straight into the hands and chest of a 49er wide receiver in the back of the end zone for a touchdown.

Maybe police need a turn and all have undercover officers to protect them. To stop this division, people who support the police receive a reward. People who want to defund the police, they ride every Saturday for a month between midnight and 6 am. If this is done, maybe there would be more respect for the police. Also, the author supports an idea by Governor Ron Desantis (FL)- a program where lawyers are provided to police officers to take BLM and Antifa members to court for assaulting the officers.

The author adds one idea, if a BLM, Antifa or MS-13 member assaults an American or murders an American, a program that provides lawyers to a hurt individual or their family to go to court. The author believes if police are defunded, then business for ADT and Simplysafe and other security companies will plummet and so will their financial earnings. Also if 911 (defund the police) centers are shut down, MedicAlert and similar companies will no longer work thus put the elderly and disabled at risk of harm. Also if a nine year old sees their grandfather have a heart attack when coming home from school, how does the child get his grandfather to the hospital if his parents are at work? What if no neighbor could help that 9 year old child? Also, there would be a lot of annoying noise pollution as burglar alarms already installed going off and there are no police to respond and turn off the alarms.

As a Psychology major, the author enjoys watching Dr. Phil and he remembers Dr. Phil telling parents: "You do not reward bad behavior" in a child. Through shows on Fox News, like Judge Jeanine, the author hears where the trouble spots, are, all Democratic cities, and it is showing crime, especially murder rising quickly due to changes in the bond system that is benefitting the criminal in these cities.

The show "Unfiltered" on Fox News is stating that the Progressives are stating that it's the Republicans who are asking to "defund the police" Where did the blame game start? Wasn't it when Adam blamed Eve for giving him the forbidden fruit? If she hadn't given it to him, he would not have eaten the forbidden fruit.

CHAPTER 2

Which Science Is Correct?

Note: Biblical Source: NIV

I wonder if the reasons the Progressives of today do not follow the science of Today as the Science of Today supports the Bible. There are many scientific concepts mentioned in the Bible before Humans discovered the concept.

Let's take a peek:
Isiah 40:22- "It is he that sits upon the circle of the earth…"

Old Scientific Theory: Earth is flat

New Scientific Theory- Earth is round, thanks to the journey of Christopher Columbus in 1492 AD. Could this be a reason some people want to take down the statue of Christopher Columbus- his journey proved a Biblical verse of the Old Testament as correct- not white supremacy?

Jeremiah 33:22- "As the host of heaven (means stars) cannot be numbered…"

Old Scientific Theory: There are 110 stars.

New Scientific Theory: There are millions of stars.

Job 26:7- "He stretched out the north over the empty place and hung the Earth upon nothing."

Old Scientific Theory: Earth held up by large animals OR Roman God Atlas.

New Scientific Theory: Free float of Earth in space.

I Corinthians 15:41- "There is one glory of the sun, there is one glory of the moon and another glory of the stars for one star differs from another star in glory"

Old Scientific Theory: Stars are the same size.

New Scientific Theory: Stars differ.

Job 38:19-20: "Where is the way that light dwells? And as for darkness where does it dwell? 20- "that though shall take it to the bound thereof and that though shall know the path to the house."

Old Scientific Theory: Light comes from a fixed source.

New Scientific Theory: Light Moves- Light Waves.

Job 28:25- "To make the weight for the winds…"

Old Scientific Theory: Air is weightless.

New Scientific Theory: Air has weight.

Ecclesiastes 1:6 "The wind goes towards the south, and turns about onto the north It whirls about continually and the wind returns again according to its circuits"

Old Scientific Theory: Winds blow straight.

New Scientific Theory: Wind blows in cyclones. Reason for the L on weather maps as well as the H

Leviticus 17:11 "For the life of the flesh is in the blood"

Old Scientific theory: If a person got bacteria in the blood, they were bled out by their medical doctors, this incudes George Washington who later died after such treatment.

New Scientific Theory: Blood is important to one's health (i.e. Blood Pressure).

2nd Samuel 22:16- "and the channels of the sea appeared, the foundations of the world discovered…"

Old Scientific Theory: Ocean floor was flat

New Scientific Theory: Ocean floor has mountains and valleys.

Job 38:16 "Has though entered into the springs of the sea…"

Old Scientific Theory: Ocean was fed by rivers and rain

New Scientific theory: Ocean has springs

Leviticus 15:13: "…. And bathe himself in running water and shall be clean"

Old Scientific theory: Wash in still water.

New Scientific theory: Wash in running water. Note: Today we know running water washes away bacteria on the hands.

The author now knows the reason the progressives do not wish to support today's science as today's science supports verses in the Bible. The author sees the dilemma the progressives are in and the reasons, many people are on the fence or lukewarm about different issues and the reason for divisions. Mask or no mask.

Vaccine or no vaccine. God or no God. Constitutional or unconstitutional.

Racism exists today or it doesn't.

However, as Jesus stated in Matthew 15: 7-9- ". Isiah was right when he prophesied about you: "These people honor me with their lips, but their hearts are far from me" 9- They worship me in vain, their teachings are merely human rules." Jesus had been talking to the Pharisees.

Doesn't the preceding also describe the politics today (2021) in the United States of America? Jesus called the crowd: "Listen and understand. What goes into someone's mouth does not defile them, but what comes out of their mouth, that is what defiles them"

12- Then the disciples came to him and asked: "Did you know the Pharisees were Offended when they heard this?"

13 Jesus replied: "Every plant that my heavenly father has not planted will be pulled up by the roots" 14- "Leave them; they are blind guides. If the blind lead the blind, both will fall into a pit"

The phrase: "Global Warming started in 2008 and was passed around like potatoes at Thanksgiving until Dallas, Texas in January 2011; two weeks before the Super Bowl (February 2011) received an unexpected snowstorm/ice storm.

Dallas in the Southern United States wasn't cold enough for this storm, many people thought, including the author, so the term was changed to: "Climate change" However, didn't there have to be climate change for the Ice Age to end?

Were there to many campfires to warm the earth to end the Ice Age? Cars and factories did not exist when the Ice Age ended.

The author keeps hearing that life is doomed in about nine years if climate change is not honored. It seems like the Progressives are concerned about the environment. Nobody brought this up, everybody wearing masks, even when outside is allegedly killing trees plus your lawn grass and when your local trees and lawn grass die, there will be no source of oxygen and more chaos. The cycle is we humans breathe in oxygen and breathe out carbon dioxide. Trees and lawn grass near us take our carbon dioxide for food and releases oxygen to us humans.

With no (lawn) grass, then there will be the end of food for grazing animals like the cow. No more cows, no more beef, which means no more hamburgers. Now the author understands the reason the Bible prophesies more vegans at the end time.

CHAPTER 3

Ill Will Criticism

Alittle joke from the author's local minister in one of her sermon's about three months ago, a man was taken into a room that had pictures- the man stated: "Ugly,

Ugly, Ugly …" The art director told him: "Sir, all the pictures in the room were done by Picasso" The man goes into a 2nd room, everything he sees is:

"Ugly, Ugly, Ugly etc." Art director tells the man: "Sir, there is nothing, but mirrors in that room" Would any of us make this same error? According to the disciple Paul, the answer is: "Yes"

What is the reason people hate being mocked? The author will agree some people might state it is cruel and may be emotionally abusive. However, the weakness we hate in ourself, when we see that weakness in another person, we hate that person. Hypothetical- What if the author had a problem dealing with anger in his past, it's possible the author could say to his friend: "The drunk at the bar must be very angry at someone, did you see many drinks he had"?

Wouldn't it be possible that the author used alcohol in the past to deal with anger?

The Progressives in their political ads say Republicans want to throw granny over the cliff for health insurance reasons. Since

January 2020, how many grandmothers have passed have passed away in the United States whether it was due to Covid or uncooperative mobs or shootings?

A Christian friend told me the ideal from the Progressives is get rid of the elders so there is no one to tell their grandchildren:

"What your teachers are teaching you in school today is incorrect" Since the Progressives did not want anyone to read the post the website on Facebook for johnnymelton/2020/04/23/milligan-71/US-2/1866, this shows fear.

I wonder how Barrack Obama, Nancy Pelosi and Chuck Schumer would react if they all went up before a military tribunal and charged with individual crimes and they all must prove themselves innocent. Would they complain that process is not fair? Would they demand their Constitutional rights? My maternal grandmother, my mother, teachers in Seaford Delaware and Scoutmasters, as well as coaches have all told me: "Life isn't fair"

Isn't that how the Progressive Democrats treated President Trump?

There are some people and cultures that believe in Karma.

However, didn't Jesus state: "One reaps what they sow"

CHAPTER 4

Cancel Culture- Cancel Today's Luxuries

Would the CEO of Coke or MLB and their family like to go without luxuries of today for nine months? If a person believes in cancel culture, they and their family do without computers, cell phones, electricity, plumbing, cars and planes OR would the CEO'S and or their family step on the brake and say: "If Woke and Cancel Culture means my family and I have to give up the luxuries of today, we won't support it" Watch Little House on the Prairie with their family to see what life was like in the 1870's in the United States. To reduce a person's high fever which included children, the patient was put into ice. Could people of today handle that? Also no computers as well as no cell phones, means no access to social media. To prevent a child from going to a friend's house or use one of these items in school, the family stays with an Amish family for 9 months. School is one building with one teacher grades K-8. If any CEO and their family takes the challenge would their gratitude of today's luxuries increase all created because of capitalism?

If this country was founded by slaves and is allegedly evil, then how has this Country stayed together for over 240 years? Didn't Jesus in Matthew 5 state:

"A kingdom divided against itself cannot stand" How was this country, the Colonists, able to defeat the British Redcoats-all powerful? How was the United States able to win both World War I and II with our Allies? If this country was allegedly evil, what is the reason people help each other after a natural disaster?

If guilt is used as an answer, it means people have a conscious.

Although Jesus stated the rain falls on the just and unjust, the author as a Christian knows that God does not bless evil. He may turn lemons into lemonade. The Nazi's of Germany or the Communists of Russia were defeated by this country.

How did this happen, if this country was evil and founded by slaves? Also if this country was evil, what was the reason for the Underground Railroad? Could slaves own property in the United States in the 1600's? According to snopes.com, black slaves were not allowed to own property or attain jobs until after the 1750's. Also according to this website there were blacks who held both white and black slaves and also Indian tribes that held slaves on their reservations.

Snopes is free to fact check itself as the website used to get this information was snopes.com . The author welcomes Sarah Palin's phrase: "A pig with lipstick is still a pig" She wasn't talking about the animal or Miss Piggy of Sesame Street; she was stating a lie can be called a myth, fable, legend, misinformation-basically it is still a lie- there are 168 synonyms for the word lie. The author means to tell a lie, not lie down on the sofa to go to sleep. There is also the lie of omission.

Fox News is asking, the Progressives and the liberal media are concentrating on cases of Covid-19 going up when hospitalization and deaths from Covid-19 are down near zero. The author of this book wonders if there are false positives for Covid-19, are those cases erased? The Progressives want to cancel culture, would they be willing to cancel statistics to show the truth? As a psychology student, the author, learned that statistics can be manipulated

Which President of this country stated: "The only thing to fear is fear itself"?

There was a post on Facebook by Kevin Noyes, 5/7/2020, accessed by the author 8/3/2021.

Do people in society know fear, worry and anxiety weaken the immune system?

Find the book titled: "Activate Your Brain" before it gets banned like Dr. Seuss.

It is our negative thinking that causes the stress chemical cortisol which leads to the call of adrenaline and a shutdown of blood flow to the pre-frontal cortex- the higher functioning part of the brain as the blood flow in the brain is going to the primitive limbic system and the fight or flight response.

The post the author wants to discuss is the following:

2000-Y2K is going to destroy everything!!

2001-Anthrax will kill us all!!

2002- West Nile Virus will kill us all

2003 Sars will kill us all!!

2005- Bird flu is going to kill us all!!

2006- E.coli is going to kill us all!!

2008- Financial collapse will kill us all!!

2009- Swine Flu will kill us all

2012- Mayan Calendar predicts world ending!!

2013- North Korea will start WW III!!

2014- Ebola Virus is going to kill us all!!

2015- ISIS is going to kill us all!!

2016- Zika Virus is going to kill us all!!

2020- Corona Virus is going to kill us all!!

Summary: Fear will kill you.

Looks like FDR was correct in predicting the future of the Democratic party and Liberal media like CNN, MSNBC, NBC, ABC and CBS News as well as many newspapers. The author is wondering if the company CEOS or Presidents/Managers never heard or forgot about the story titled: "Boy Who Cried Wolf" It brings an interesting story from beliefnet.com. There was a man talking to children of various ages and maturity levels. He told them all a story of his past that his doctor told him he had stage 4 untreatable brain cancer and he had 3-6 months to live. Being rich, he quit his job, bought a yacht and sailed around the world to see the seven wonders of the world. At the end of the story he states:

"It has been 10 years and I'm still living!!" The children in the story were his children, grandchildren, nephews and nieces at a family reunion. Just because a person has a serious virus, cancer or heart problems doesn't mean that is what will kill the person. Don't people die in natural disasters, man-made disasters, car accidents, plane accidents, train accidents, shipping accidents, drowning, struck by lightning and other reasons?

There is Only one person who knows how and when a person's life will end.

CHAPTER 5

Confusion

Do the words intent and motive have the same definition? Should a person cower in fear, every time the phrase: "I will kill you" is uttered in the United States of America? The Bible states to: "fear the Lord" Is that the same type of fear that one has with snakes? A person states "they fear snakes"

Wouldn't that type of fear drive a person away from God and the Bible? Couldn't "Fear the Lord" mean worship the Lord or respect the Lord?

When the author was growing up, he heard the following phrase from his mother, Scoutmaster and teachers: "Sticks and stones will break my bones, but words will never hurt me" One day, while watching TBN with a friend, a TV pastor said:

"A bone can be stitched up, once a word is said it is out there for good and can not be taken back. A good analogy is can a person put toothpaste back in the tube it just came out of without cutting the tube? Forty years ago, if the author's middle brother told his parents: "I will do grass on Saturday" that was okay as the parents knew grass meant lawn- he will cut the grass Saturday. In today's society, the phrase "I will do grass on Saturday" would have a parent on edge.

The rule, "no prayer in school" Does prayer mean hope? "I hope I will pass this math test" In some cultures, saying thank you is considered a prayer as a person is showing gratitude. Does this mean primary teachers can no longer teach manners- No praying in school?

The author used the Internet and put the phrase: "No preying" That phrase means not taking advantage of others. Looks like: "No preying" and "No praying" offset each other and it reminds the author of a past dream:

He was the head coach for a football team, his offense was on the field.

Neither team had any time outs. First play, ten yard pass down the middle of the field, then a brawl started and with 19 seconds, an official throws a penalty flag which stops the clock at 19 seconds- offsetting penalties, ten seconds are run off leaving 9 seconds left in game, time for one more play and that play was a 35 yard touchdown pass to win the game. Opposing team players and coaches all alleged that the author told his team to cause a penalty to stop the clock.

Why wasn't there a dispute before that last play?

The sport committee couldn't make a ruling, so it turned out to be a local court case. The author saw the judge enter the room to sit on his bench. The first words spoken by the judge was: "The Sports committee needs to take a sentence out of its bylaws and it is the sentence: "If the committee can't solve a conflict, it will go to a local judge, courts are just too busy for this" This is the only football case the judge will hear. The judge hears the testimony of a couple witnesses and sees the video of the game- last minute of game to end of game, then the judge retires to his chambers. Five minutes later, the judge comes out and rules on the case.

The judge tells the plaintiff - opposing coach: "Your players participated in the brawl, they could have all walked away and let the clock run out" The judge checked the rulebook and the officials did everything correct, so the last play, the TD play counts and the author's team wins the game"

What is the reason a person can tell a dream or nightmare to another, even after years passed, however cannot remember details of a street accident that occurred the week before? Both happen suddenly and unexpected. We all need to remember the phrases: "Innocent until proven guilty" and: "Guilty beyond a reasonable doubt" in the United States.

The author wants to thank a psychology professor (female) who showed her class how to tell when a person is lying. Most people cannot control this:

Verbal language and Non Verbal Language Disagree. This means a person says:

"Yes", but shakes their head "No" or the person says: "No" and nods yes. The only people not affected by this are adults who got away with a major lie to their parents when a child and excellent poker players- the Bluff.

The author's dream story has the word "bench" that could mean bench/stool/chair or "bench" in sports means: "not play a person"

The word retires in the dream story means: went. People retire at 65 years old has another meaning. The author has heard the following phrase multiple times: "If one tells the truth, they don't have to worry about remembering items"

The author was eating at a restaurant, the other day, and saw a sign that stated:

"No shoes, No shirt, No pants, No service" For the author the confusing part is "No pants"- what if a man wears shorts or a lady wears a dress?

The author wants readers to try an experiment to show the reason for closed shoes when outside. The author asks: School children and adults try talking with their mouth closed- that is lockjaw, another name for tetanus and that could happen stepping on some glass or a rusty nail when barefoot. What would be better for a child? A snake with a yellow band crawl across the barefoot of your eight year old. Would sandals protect him better or would sneakers be the best protection?

When the author was in Boy Scouts, he learned if a snake had a yellow band-caution. If the yellow band touched a red band-danger: coral snake which is poisonous. The above scene shows reasons for rules, instructions and even laws-for our own protection.

The author wonders what if members of a Marxist group were to feel the sting of pain when trying to get a peaceful protest out of control. What if someone saw a man loading a gun and was getting ready to shoot into a crowd and what if a patriotic American were to give a good kick to the back, either side of the spine to hit a nerve in that person and let them feel the sting of pain which would cause that person to drop their weapon.

Is the American Constitution a social contract? The author checked, both the Declaration of Independence and the Constitution are both social contracts.

Since the author was born in Delaware, how could the representative Caesar Rodney, sign for the author when his parents have not been born yet? If colonists/citizens disagreed about this document in 1800, it would have been abolished, just like the Articles of Confederation ended.

The author learned from a book written by Dr. James Dobson that a deceitful phrase started in 1966 which contributed to the sexual immorality of today and the phrase is: "God is Dead" The author of this book is now 55 years old with a BA in Psychology. If the phrase: "God is Dead" was true, then how was the author and everyone since then born? The author wonders if that phrase was true, what is the reason for no trees, desert only around the whole earth. If that phrase was true, how do all the cycles still work today in 2021 AD as they did in 1500 AD?

Earlier in this book it showed that beliefs in science change.

If the Constitution is a social contract, then no preying by the Biden administration of today, especially upon Jews and Christians, no preying means taking advantage of another person or group of people, this would include Jews and Christians.

Also teaching Critical Race Theory, White Supremacy and brainwashing are forms of gaslighting- extreme emotional abuse. Romans 13 of the New Testament gives the answer about reparations, the only thing WE owe our neighbor is Love. The scoutmaster of the author who grew up in Southern Delaware was: "Christian Love" "Christian Love" meant sharing your time and/or things, if you have extra, with others. The policies of the Biden administration violates much of James of the New Testament.

The author just checked, according to three dental websites wearing face masks can cause dental problems especially bacteria growth in the mouth and dry mouth. There is now a phrase: "mask mouth" coined after "meth mouth" Due to bacteria growth in the mouth it can cause bad breath. Also webmd stated that dental problems (bacterium gingivitis which causes bleeding gums) could signal future problems with dementia and Alzheimer's Disease. The author's mother had Alzheimer's for about four years before dying in 2010. This author remembers his mother getting a root canal while growing up.

Would government officials that ask for mask mandates in public be willing to pay out of their own pockets for future dental health and neurological health for people who followed their masks mandates?

Government phrase: "Run, hide, fight" goes against the fight/flight response of the human brain. Hiding creates cortisol, a stress chemical and negative thinking while hiding due to fear can create problems in the brain. If government officials tell their local police to "stand down", maybe there are patriotic Americans that will make a physical stand against members of a Marxist or Antifa group. If Government officials know there are patriotic persons who will come to the defense of others, they won't tell the local police to "stand down"

The author believes: "People have the right to protect self, others or property"

The author agrees there is a lot of deception in today's world. Pastor Rick Warren of TBN announced on Sunday August 15, 2021 that there are a lot of Artificial in today's world- artificial sweeteners, artificial meat, artificial knowledge like robots and even artificial churches. An artificial church is like religious cults of today which proves that Jesus was correct about false prophets, a good example is Jim Jones getting 900 people to kill themselves with poisonous Kool-Aid. A God of Love would not ask anyone to kill themselves to glorify him or his son Jesus.

Confusion can cause errors/mistakes especially in communications. The author is sure, that many readers, if not all, whether adult or child, have been embarrassed with "the cat got your tongue phenomenon" Also a man catching a woman falling near a river (rescue) might look like a romantic embrace to a younger person. It took the 10th angle for the author to see why the substitute referee's call was upheld. Also isn't it very hard to think and concentrate when a person has a pounding headache? Couldn't a pounding headache be caused by a clenched jaw while gritting one's teeth. Gritting one's teeth can be a reaction to distress, anxiety, worry and fear.

Confusion/mistakes can lead to new inventions or new ideas. The author poured (pop) soda on his pancakes instead of syrup one morning. Maybe someone will further that idea and come up with soda flavored pancakes. There was a man in the late 1700's tries a machine that was aimed at stopping press smears in a hot humid summer in a city like Philadelphia. The idea didn't work as planned-smears still occurred as it was tried in several buildings, however someone noticed the printing press rooms were the coolest in the building where that machine was tried. That mistake led to the air conditioner. A young boy one afternoon around CA in the early 1900's had a drink of soda and sugar with a stick to stir while playing outside. The boy forgot to clean up the porch before going to bed. That night, temperatures went below freezing and that is how the popsicle was created.

It was not called a popsicle at first.

People were willing to share and try their ideals due to capitalism. If this country didn't have capitalism, we wouldn't have air conditioning nor the popsicle as we know them today.

The author remembers a time around fifth grade where the bully in the class would ask him: "May I copy your math problems?" If the answer was: "NO", a fight broke out. Telling the teacher was considered "snitching" The author learned from a male classmate which was do the assignment incorrectly, for example in math- add where it says to multiply. Next day, at recess tell the teacher "I believe my math was done incorrectly, believe there was too much noise in my house that distracted me. I wish to stay inside during recess to redo my math homework. I may not be the only person in class who made these errors." The bullies learned that their classmates could give them incorrect answers for homework and the bully can not complain to anyone. If Mrs. Smith asks: "Sean, did Earle copy your math assignment?. If Sean answers: "Yes", he is answering the teacher's question and not snitching. The author and his classmates would try to get their teacher to ask a question if a bully was bothering them.

CHAPTER 6

Conclusion

If Progressives and many people believe in White Supremacy, the website statista.com shows that over 84% of homosexuals are white and white. Is there a danger of them getting cancelled out: cancel culture. These values rose greatly after 1977.

If the progressives and some people in society believe there is more than two genders, the author heard 57 from a source not remembered, then which one can give birth. Can a rooster lay an egg or can a bull give milk? If anyone wants to try, make sure no red is being worn. Which genders have hot flashes and menopause? How much alcohol is acceptable per gender?

Finally, risks of high estrogen levels in males: stroke, blood clots, diabetes, certain cancers (i.e. male breast cancer), ED, infertility, dementia, depression, and osteoporosis. By the way marijuana increases the estrogen level in the body, possible reason for seeming "stoned" (form of dementia).

Risks of high testosterone levels in females: excess body hair, especially facial hair, balding, acne, decreased breast size, deepening of voice, increased muscle mass, irregular menstrual cycles, changes in mood, infertility, obesity, insulin resistance, low levels of HDL (good cholesterol), elevated Triglycerides, High LDL (

bad cholesterol) and High Blood Pressure. Are puberty blockers or anti-sex hormones still a good idea?

Six different medical sites agreed about the preceding health problems- 3 for males, 3 for females. All six websites state that both men and women have both testosterone and estrogen. Men need estrogen for strong bones. Too much of anything can be hurtful. Looks like the Progressives as well as some members of today's society want to tell Science/Biology what is correct, while the rest of society wants to hear what Science states is correct as of today. No wonder this world is chaotic, however by learning the truth WE can eliminate this chaos.

Many of us complain about different things like the weather when camping, hiking or fishing, what is the reason for the strong lightening storms, or traffic delays when one is already ten minutes late to work or the cost of items (Why is the electric bill) so high? Maybe we complain to others and possibly we also complain to God. Wouldn't God want us to be thankful? What if Henry Ford didn't make the first car, could our recreational and professional lives be different, if this society still used horse and buggy? Electric bill too high? What if electricity had never been discovered? Many luxury items of today would be thrown out the window.

Do we want to teach people, especially our children how to critique God? Last week, the author found some hand written notes in a notebook about a personal incident that occurred about 1995, July 4th holiday. The author whose first name is Fred, made a mistake on a simple task setting up a table for the BBQ. He was hard on himself calling himself an idiot 1,000 times in 3 hours before drifting off to sleep in his parent's guest room. The next morning, the author heard a voice:

"Fred, you call yourself an idiot, you call God one" The author being between sleep and wakefulness talked back to the voice: "If true for me, true for others"

The word others has a double meaning. If I call John Doe an idiot, I am telling God his creation of John Doe is idiotic. If John Doe calls Fred an idiot, John Doe is informing God that his creation of Fred is idiotic. The theme to the incident is:

It is actions that are dumb, stupid, foolish, idiotic, not people. Shouldn't we be teaching people, especially children to respect God, not to critique God.

www.ingramcontent.com/pod-product-compliance
Lightning Source LLC
Chambersburg PA
CBHW050755250726
48662CB00005B/2234